EDM

Other titles in the *Music Scene* series include:

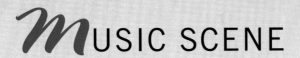

MUSIC SCENE

EDM

Jamuna Carroll

ReferencePoint
Press®

San Diego, CA

© 2020 ReferencePoint Press, Inc.
Printed in the United States

For more information, contact:
ReferencePoint Press, Inc.
PO Box 27779
San Diego, CA 92198
www.ReferencePointPress.com

LIBRARY OF CONGRESS CATALOGING-IN-PUBLICATION DATA

Name: Carroll, Jamuna, author.
Title: EDM/by Jamuna Carroll.
Description: San Diego, CA: ReferencePoint Press, [2019] | Series: Music
  Scene | Audience: Grade 9 to 12. | Includes bibliographical references and
  index.
Identifiers: LCCN 2019016243 (print) | LCCN 2019016470 (ebook) | ISBN
  9781682826409 (eBook) | ISBN 9781682826393 (hardback)
Subjects: LCSH: Electronic dance music—History and criticism—Juvenile
  literature.
Classification: LCC ML3540.5 (ebook) | LCC ML3540.5 .C37 2019 (print) | DDC
  781.648—dc23
LC record available at https://lccn.loc.gov/2019016243

$\mathcal{C}$ONTENTS

By Young People, for Young People

Electronic dance music (EDM) is one of the newest music genres, having only become widely popular in the first two decades of the 2000s. Although EDM is technically a subgenre of electronic music, in the United States the two terms are used interchangeably. With a repetitive beat and catchy hooks, EDM is also called dance music or club music, because it is meant to get people dancing. While the genre began with techno, electro, and house music, today it has countless subcategories—from electro-pop and dubstep to moombahton and tech house.

Whatever style they play, EDM DJs seamlessly blend one track into the next, creating a mix that ebbs and flows. EDM is intended to provide an emotional experience for listeners as they dance their troubles away. Tom Breihan, senior editor at the music website Stereogum, says, "Dance music is about transcendence, about the moment of epiphany"[1] that occurs while listening. To create a group bonding experience, DJs who are tuned in to the crowd drop energetic tracks at key moments and slow down the set at others.

From DJ to Producer

Although *DJ* stands for "disc jockey," they are rarely called disc jockeys anymore. Nowadays, *disc jockey* usually refers only to radio hosts whereas a DJ is anyone who plays recorded music for a live audience. Most DJs do more than just play one track after another, though. Some create impressive mash-ups, which are the simultaneous playing of two or more songs. One DJ, for example, mashed up Marshmello's dance track "Happier" with the song "Sunflower" by rappers Post Malone and Swae Lee; it got 109,000 likes in its first twelve weeks on YouTube.

Mash-ups illustrate how DJs have expanded their role into that of producer. Unlike bands or hip-hop acts, who hire record producers to enhance their tracks, nearly all successful DJs serve as their own producers, too. An early example is a DJ named Jeff Mills, more popularly known as the Wizard. In the 1990s, he released unfinished tracks that artists had to layer with other songs to complete them. Essentially, the Wizard made tracks that turned *other* DJs into production wizards. Another way that DJs act as producers is by remixing, or reworking, existing songs in their own style. They may also "sample" music, or reuse a song's bass line, instrumental section, or vocals, in their own track. Then, using computers, synthesizers, drum machines, or other musical equipment, producers finish composing their tunes. Sometimes they are hired to produce, or add their own flair to, other musicians' grooves.

Music journalists Bill Brewster and Frank Broughton write in their book *Last Night a DJ Saved My Life* that producing allows DJs to remain on top of their game. "Making their own records, or reconstructing those made by others, is a natural extension of the club DJ's trade, a way to put [their] creative stamp on the world," the authors point out. "It's how a DJ can most convincingly claim artist status."[2]

New Developments Allow Younger DJs to Excel

Technology has significantly changed the world of DJing. DJ decks used to consist of turntables that played vinyl records, which artists lugged around in crates. Today decks commonly

In the past, DJs lugged crates of records and turntables to gigs. With today's technology, EDM artists often use a laptop and DJ mixer to create their sounds.

feature a laptop, DJ controller, mixer, or CDJs that play CDs or digital music. No longer do producers need expensive recording equipment or a dedicated music studio. Nearly anyone can create electronic music using computer programs such as Reason, FL Studio, Ableton Live, or Logic Pro. Furthermore, EDM hopefuls can promote their own music online without first having a record label sponsor them.

Because of these advancements, even young teens like Martin Garrix, Madeon, and Hardwell (who landed his first record deal at age fourteen) have hit it big as producers before they were even old enough to attend clubs where their music is played. One reason that young people are attracted to electronic music is because the genre relies heavily on technology, and young people are a tech-savvy age group. Indeed, of the twelve highest-earning DJs in 2018, nearly half are in their twenties.

From Illegal Parties to Top of the Pop Charts

Dance music fans, too, are overwhelmingly young. The largest segment of listeners (33 percent) comprises ages eighteen to twenty-four, according to a study by Nielsen Entertainment. This is not surprising, considering that EDM began with teenage DJs who produced tracks at home. Soon, young DJs spun records for their friends at illegal underage parties called raves. Attendees danced all night—or until authorities raided the event. Music journalist Michaelangelo Matos notes, "Rave was America's last great outlaw musical subculture: created by kids, for kids, designed to be impenetrable to adults."[3] But what was once underground eventually grew to be mainstream.

It is no wonder, then, that *Rolling Stone* magazine has called EDM "the defining youth culture of the 2010s."[4] Electronic music has influenced other music genres, as well as fashion and dance, and has taken over rock magazines, country music acts, pop charts, and video games. Whereas young people used to have to search to find where EDM was being played, today they do not need to leave home to hear it. Club music is widely streamed and easily available for purchase. Although electronic music appeals to fans of all ages, its roots still have a hold in younger generations, who, in turn, are steering it into the future.

"Rave was America's last great outlaw musical subculture: created by kids, for kids, designed to be impenetrable to adults."[3]

—Michaelangelo Matos, music journalist

The Roots of EDM

Music has long featured electronic sounds. Music professor Daniel Warner traces the first electronic music record back to 1960: *Kontakte* by German composer Karlheinz Stockhausen. Punctuated by reverberating pulses, discordant piano notes, and scattered drum beats, it was a musical experiment unlike anything before it; however, it is not electronic music as we now know it, the kind that gets heads bobbing and bodies bouncing. *That* type of music sprang specifically from 1970s disco and funk music and 1980s synthpop, or pop music that features a synthesizer instrument.

Because EDM tracks are so often borrowed from and built onto one another, it is difficult to identify the first electronic music song. But most music scholars agree EDM was inspired by disco music, particularly Donna Summer's hypnotic hit "I Feel Love" (1977). Disco features the use of drum machines, electronic instruments, and a steady beat to get people dancing, just like EDM. "I Feel Love" was revolutionary for its futuristic synthesizer (synth) sounds and its production technique. To make it, the producers used a synthesizer to electronically generate every sound separately, including each note of each chord. Then, a very talented sound engineer synchronized, or synched, all parts of the track together in a way that even the synthesizer's inventor did not know was possible. In this way, "I Feel Love" introduced the synth into modern music and kickstarted the development of EDM. Music critic Bill Brewster sums up the tune this way: "Released 40 years ago, yet still somehow managing to sound like the future even today, it's dance music's Year Zero; the song that started our journey through electronic disco, house, techno and beyond."[5]

The funk bands Parliament and Funkadelic (which sometimes played together as P-Funk) also influenced early EDM artists. Spearheaded by singer George Clinton, P-Funk took the funk

Donna Summer, known as "The Queen of Disco," performs in 1978. Most music scholars agree EDM was inspired by disco music and its steady dance beats.

of soul singer James Brown and his contemporaries to another level, electrifying funk by using a synth to imitate a bass guitar and other instruments.

The synth's electronic sound was integral to synthpop, too. The synthpop act that most influenced early club music was the German electronic band Kraftwerk. Calling its style "robot pop," the band played solely electronic sounds using drum machines, vocoders (machines that electronically distort vocals), and custom-built sequencers (which are used to edit music as it is performed live). Music reviewer Jude Rogers explains the far-reaching impact Kraftwerk had on EDM. "Kraftwerk's beats laid the foundations for club music: for hip-hop, synth-pop, techno and house,"[6] she notes. Other esteemed acts, like Telex from Belgium and Yellow Magic Orchestra from Japan, also paved the way for EDM.

"Kraftwerk's beats laid the foundations for club music."[6]

—Jude Rogers, music reviewer

Techno, the First Electronic Dance Music

The sounds of disco, funk, and synthpop all converged in the late 1970s in a legendary radio show in Detroit, Michigan. It was hosted by a disc jockey called the Electrifying Mojo, who presided over Detroit's underground music scene. He introduced to his legion of fans music from local, not-yet-known DJs as well as rarely played tracks from more established celebrities, like Prince. Among his many fans were a group of high school friends named Juan Atkins, Derrick May, and Kevin Saunderson, who experimented with records in their bedrooms, merging the sounds they heard the Electrifying Mojo play. Their extraordinary new style, which became known as techno, blended synthpop and disco with funk and sometimes added distorted vocals. Atkins and his friend Richard Davis, who worked together under the DJ name Cybotron, produced the techno single "Alleys of

How a Detroit Radio DJ Promoted Electronic Music

One radio disc jockey known as the Electrifying Mojo was instrumental in pushing electronic music forward. A former US Army radio DJ during the Vietnam War, the Electrifying Mojo got his own nightly radio show in Detroit. Famous for his voice but rarely appearing in public, the mysterious DJ began each show with sounds that supposedly represented a spaceship that brought him to Earth from a distant planet.

During his extraordinary three-hour-long show, he spun underground records by artists who ultimately inspired the creation of techno music. For instance, the Electrifying Mojo often featured sets by Detroit native Ken Collier, a flamboyant DJ who could revive a dead dance floor within seconds. Collier's eclectic mix of disco and soul influenced the young DJs who would soon pioneer the genre of techno. Collier's protégé Stacey "Hotwaxx" Hale had groundbreaking mixes aired on the show, too. Collier and Hale became known as the godfather and godmother of dance music. Hale says, "We were setting the tone for techno. We didn't know that's what we were doing, but we did [it]."

The Electrifying Mojo was considered an underground cult hero, first because he gave a platform to artists like Collier and Hale, and then by playing the first tracks by techno pioneer Juan Atkins and his friends. By sharing early techno on the radio, he introduced the genre to many new fans in Detroit and beyond.

Quoted in Ashley Zlatopolsky, "The Roots of Techno: Detroit's Club Scene, 1973–1985," *Red Bull Music Academy Daily*, July 31, 2014. http://daily.redbullmusicacademy.com.

Your Mind" in 1981. The same year, the Detroit group known as A Number of Names released "Sharevari," which sampled a Kraftwerk song. Both singles have been celebrated as the first techno track, and both got their radio debut courtesy of the Electrifying Mojo.

Early techno artists hailed from Detroit, where the once-booming automotive industry had imploded, plunging the city from prosperity into ruin. As May explained in 1988, "Techno is the sound of young Detroit: built by machines, and driven by despair."[7] Where drugs, gangs, and poverty reigned, techno served as an escape for listeners and for the DJs who created it. The teens recorded tracks under the Metroplex label that Atkins started in 1985. May's roommate Eddie "Flashin'" Fowlkes brought the label its first hit with "Goodbye Kiss," a techno record with a funky soul sound.

"Techno is the sound of young Detroit: built by machines, and driven by despair."[7]

—Derrick May, techno pioneer

The young DJs' tracks were featured on a seminal compilation in 1988 called *Techno! The New Dance Sound of Detroit*. Due to the album's success, techno spread to other cities and Europe. What followed was techno's second wave, when the genre was further developed by US artists such as Underground Resistance and Carl Craig, Canadians Ritchie Hawtin and John Acquiviva, and UK techno DJs.

Electro and House Follow Closely on Techno's Heels

Another hub for EDM was New York, where early hip-hop DJs were also inspired by synthpop and funk. In 1982 producer Afrika Bambaataa isolated the beat from one of Kraftwerk's songs, married it with the melody from another Kraftwerk track, and added a drum machine. This produced an innovative, funky sound with a prominent drumbeat and vocoder-distorted vocals. What he named "Planet Rock" was the first track of a genre called electro, and it was so influential that it ranked number 240 on *Rolling Stone*'s top 500 songs in history as of 2010. Electro was quickly picked up by other New York DJs, including Grandmaster Flash, Warp 9, and Hashim. As the electro scene expanded, MCs rapped over tracks, breakdancers performed gravity-defying flips, and graffiti artists painted to the beat.

Around the same time, the genre of house music was born in Chicago. Both techno and house energized the dance floor, with a fast tempo around 128 beats per minute (bpm). That was ideal for Frankie Knuckles, a DJ with a residency (a regular gig) at the Warehouse, a gay club in Chicago. There, he spliced sounds of disco classics, Philadelphia soul, and R&B (rhythm and blues) with synthpop, creating high-energy sets. Although he was not the first house music producer, he became known for the style, which was named "house" after the Warehouse. In his sets, Frankie Knuckles played house tracks by local producers, including Chip E.'s "Jack Trax" and "Music Is the Key" by J.M. Silk.

House music had a message that resonated with minority groups. Its lyrics often highlighted frustrations with racism, sexism, and oppression. House DJs were mostly African American artists from Chicago and included people like Derrick Carter, Ron Trent, and Cajmere (also called Green Velvet). Another key figure was a Puerto Rican artist called DJ Sneak, who was regarded as a global ambassador of house music.

Electronica Goes to Britain

Although electronic music emerged in the United States, it did not catch on there for years. Dance music did not appeal to mainstream, white Americans, partly due to the fact that it was created and largely played by African Americans. Furthermore, house music was shunned because it originated in gay clubs. It was not until the 1990s that house music became more widespread through East Coast artists like Masters at Work and Danny Tenaglia. On the West Coast, it infiltrated San Francisco through the illustrious Wicked crew and, later, Doc Martin. Music historians note that racism and homophobia prevented electronic music from being accepted earlier.

Europe, however, was quick to adopt EDM. Artists in Britain, Germany, and Holland expanded on the sounds they imported from the United States. In the late 1980s and 1990s, house and techno songs entered the UK music charts. Farley "Jackmaster" Funk and Jesse Saunders, who collaborated on the first international house hit, "Love Can't Turn Around," were among the first American house DJs to earn recognition in the UK. In many cases,

The Significance of Digital Music in EDM

One of the most important technological advancements in dance music is the creation of digital music. Early DJs worked with vinyl records, which are heavy, breakable, and can warp in hot weather. Then some artists tried CDs, which are hardier but still damageable. When music started becoming available in digital formats (such as mp3s) in the 1990s, many artists were willing to leave their records behind.

Jace Clayton, also known as DJ Rupture, provides an example of why digital music was so useful. He was headed to a gig in 2002 when his van was totaled in a crash that destroyed all one hundred of his best records. After that, he switched to a digital vinyl system (DVS), which lets DJs use a turntable, mixer, and vinyl record to "spin" mp3s. DVS works and sounds the same as a traditional system, but records can be easily backed up on drives, just in case. Alternatively, some DJs use two or more CDJ players plugged into a mixer. As the name implies, CDJs play CDs, but also digital music from memory sticks or cards. For example, the superstar DJ David Guetta uses a single thirty-two-gigabyte memory stick to hold all his music for a show.

In some cases, DJs do not even need those items. Some popular DJ software has integrated with music-streaming sites. Artists using Serato DJ, for instance, can play and mix songs from the sites SoundCloud and Tidal, giving them access to underground tracks. With digital music, DJs can perform without bringing music, giving them more flexibility and portability.

American DJs moved to Europe to pursue careers because they were still relatively unknown at home.

Back then, electronic music was clumped together under the term *electronica*. Eventually producers added their own twist, generating countless subgenres. For example, when the artists Phuture and Ron Hardy used a synth to create squelchy sounds over house music, they forged what became known as acid house. In Chicago, jazz musician Larry Heard added a dreamy instrumental melody to house tracks, pioneering the genre of deep house. From France came the aptly named French house. Other musicians fused techno and electro with house, giving birth to tech house and electro house, respectively. Another style, progressive house, was recently revived by European DJs, including the Swedish producer Alesso. Progressive house is described by music journalist Dom Phillips as "hard but tuneful, banging but thoughtful, uplifting and trancey British house . . . mad but melodic music that makes you want to dance."[8]

One spinoff of house music, called trance, emerged circa 1990 in Germany. Meant to lull listeners into a trance, songs usually build to a crescendo, then the producer fades out the beat to highlight the melody before resuscitating the beat more intensely. Some trance pioneers include DJs Ferry Corsten, from the Netherlands; Paul van Dyk, the first DJ to be ranked number one by the dance music magazine *Mixmag*; and Armin Van Buuren, whose *State of Trance* radio show had 41 million weekly listeners in 2019. As trance spread, it opened the doors for today's trance kingpins like Above and Beyond, arguably the UK's most famous DJ act.

Electronic Music Paves the Way for Rave Culture

Still, when EDM was emerging, few clubs were willing to book electronic music DJs because fans were too young to attend. Therefore, young Brits began throwing illegal parties, known as raves, where they could blast club music. To do so, they often broke into warehouses or airplane hangars, where they set up temporary decks. DJs also played in fields or other outdoor sites where they would not attract the attention of police.

DJs Paul Oakenfold, Danny Rampling, and their friends legitimized raves in Britain by opening electronic music clubs in the late 1980s. Their clubs blared underground styles that no one had heard before. One was Balearic house music imported from the Spanish island of Ibiza, the nightclub capital of the world (and one of the Balearic Islands, hence the name). Soon, New York DJs brought raves to the United States. At these free-for-alls, kids as young as twelve danced all night. Drug use was rampant, as the overall effect of the pulsing beats and strobing lights—as well as the energy to dance all night—was enhanced when people took psychoactive drugs like MDMA (ecstasy) or LSD (acid). Unfortunately, with this came the dangers of overdose, rape, and even death.

Throughout the 1990s, EDM events multiplied, and the music spawned a rave culture that went global. "Ravers" donned baggy streetwear and tennis shoes that let them dance comfortably. They accessorized with colorful beaded jewelry, blinking lights, and referees' whistles that they blew along to the beat. Ravewear was so creative—and outrageous—that it soon was being modeled on fashion runways.

New dance styles emerged, too. Ravers pioneered what became known as liquid dancing, rolling their bodies like ocean waves. By incorporating light-up props into the party, they also were the first to practice glowstick dancing and glowstick spinning. These were precursors to the dance performances seen at EDM events today, such as light-up hula hooping and fire spinning.

Electronic Music Hits the Charts

EDM broke onto the mainstream American music scene when the Prodigy, an electronic rock band, had two songs reach the Top 40 in 1997. Finally, electronic music was on America's radar. Unlike most EDM artists, whose shows consisted of blending into the background behind their decks, the Prodigy put on a lively show. "They were rock stars, and they carried themselves as such, thrashing around onstage rather than letting the spotlight go anywhere else,"[9] says music journalist Tom Breihan. As a result, the Prodigy's style of electronica caught on with rock and punk fans.

The Prodigy's triumph was followed up by that of another artist, bassist Fatboy Slim. He sampled tracks from the 1960s and 1970s by Sly and the Family Stone, the James Gang, Camille Yarbrough, and Five Man Electrical Band. Audiences loved it; by 1999 he had three tracks ranked in the top 40 of *Billboard*'s Alternative Songs chart, including a number 2 hit ("Praise You").

The Prodigy, an electronic rock band, had two songs reach the Top 40 in 1997. The Prodigy's style of electronica caught on with rock and punk fans.

This was all the more impressive considering that electronica DJs did not usually break onto music charts at all. He even received two Grammy Award nominations. Soon, Americans saw the rise of electronica artists such as the Chemical Brothers, Sasha and John Digweed, and Moby, as well as Sandra Collins, the first female superstar DJ.

Many Spinoff Genres

Meanwhile in Europe, new EDM genres were developing, such as hardcore. Not to be confused with the punk or metal genres of the same name, hardcore EDM is characterized by sped-up beats and vocals—sometimes topping 200 bpm—that sometimes sound cartoonish. The style lends itself to head banging and mosh dancing.

Some DJs took hardcore sounds and blended them with reggae, hip-hop, and even jazz. This is how the genre of drum and bass (also called jungle) was born. Averaging 160 to 180 bpm, drum and bass is faster than house or techno, and sometimes harder to dance to. UK drum and bass pioneer Goldie influenced legions of artists with the release of his debut album *Timeless* (1995), which in 2011 was named one of the top 50 events in dance music history by the influential Manchester, England, newspaper the *Guardian*. Another master of drum and bass is Andy C, whose "double drop" style involves playing two tracks such that both bass lines hit simultaneously.

Other genres forged in the 1990s include UK garage, breakbeat, glitch, and trip hop. Some of this music is not necessarily easy to dance to, but it nonetheless captured the imagination of later DJs. Aphex Twin, for example, made experimental ambient music that many now-famous EDM artists, including Deadmau5 and Skrillex, credit as among their greatest influences.

Backlash

As EDM became more popular, there was pushback from parents and politicians concerned that it promoted drug use and other dangerous behavior. For instance, one illegal rave in 1992 attracted up to forty thousand people to Castlemorton Common in England. It grew so big that police were unable to shut it down. In response, British lawmakers in 1994 prohibited outdoor gatherings where people listen to "repetitive beats"; the law also permitted authorities to confiscate cars and sound systems at such events.

The law sparked huge demonstrations; tens of thousands of people marched in protest. Some hosted what were essentially dance-ins, erecting sound systems in the streets of London. A few artists tried to circumvent the law by creating music that technically skirted the law's description. For example, when the DJ duo Autechre released the track "Flutter," they noted it had "been programmed in such a way that no bars contain identical beats and can therefore be played under the proposed new law."[10] Autechre added a satirical warning that DJs might need a lawyer and a music expert to prove that the song could be played legally.

In the United States, critics of both electronic music and the raves where it was featured took note of the British law and sought to pass their own. American authorities tried to crack down on the genre by classifying electronic music venues as crack houses, or as buildings used to manufacture or sell illegal drugs. A federal law from 2003, for example, holds building owners and event promoters responsible if their raves promote drug use.

"No Going Back"

Despite laws targeting EDM, the genre flourished. In 1994 an acclaimed music event in England called the Glastonbury Festival featured a set by the DJ duo Orbital that proved to be game-changing. Although rock and folk musicians starred at the festival, Orbital won over a crowd that was skeptical of electronic music, drawing an audience of forty thousand to their acid house and techno set. Furthermore, the festival was televised for the first

DJ duo Orbital performs in 2009. In 1994, Orbital won over a festival crowd that was skeptical of electronic music, drawing an audience of forty thousand to their acid house and techno set.

time, showing all viewers, from music critics to people who had never heard of electronica, that dance music crowds had reached epic proportions. Also, contrary to warnings about the dangers of raves, the festival looked not much different from a regular rock concert. "What was previously underground made it on to one of the big stages, and there was no going back," says Glastonbury's organizer, Michael Eavis. "The buzz had been around the raves . . . for years. But [dance music] needed a showcase to make it legal."[11] Glastonbury served that role, and the next year got its first dance tent, a stage featuring electronic music.

EDM became recognized as a legitimate form of music at the turn of the twenty-first century. At the 1999 Grammy Awards, the DJ duo Daft Punk was nominated for best dance recording for "Around the World" alongside pop star Madonna's "Ray of Light," which was a techno-pop track with hints of trance. "Ray of Light" won best dance track, introducing electronic music to scores of pop fans.

Around 2000, British DJs started tinkering with the darker sounds of drum and bass and UK garage, creating a subgenre known as dubstep. Featuring deep, wobbly bass lines that sound like "wubwubwub," dubstep is slowed down to about 75 bpm. A seminal moment for this subgenre came in 2006, when disc jockey Mary Anne Hobbs hosted a two-hour set by dubstep pioneers on her radio show, which aired on the BBC (Britain's national public broadcaster). The special edition "Dubstep Warz" featured seven sets by Skream, Hatcha, Digital Mystikz, Kode9, and other visionaries. It was widely credited for bringing the emerging genre to the forefront. "It brings tears to my eyes," recalls Hobbs. "If, as a broadcaster, you can deliver one show with the cultural & historical impact of this one in a lifetime . . . it's a miracle."[12] By 2008 the dubstep track "Eastern Jam," which uniquely samples

> "If, as a broadcaster, you can deliver one show with the cultural & historical impact of [the "Dubstep Warz" show] in a lifetime . . . it's a miracle."[12]
>
> —Mary Anne Hobbs, radio disc jockey

an Indian song from a Bollywood film, reached number one on the UK dance charts and was named one of the best dubstep tracks of all time.

While early dubstep featured slow instrumental mixes, artists like England's Rusko and Canada's Excision pushed it in a different direction, adding beats that dropped especially hard and fast. American DJs took off with this style of dubstep. It paved the way for trap music, which sounds like electro house blended with rap. Hard-hitting dubstep also set the stage for the bass-bouncing style of future bass that is played by the Chainsmokers and other acts.

Over the years, electronic music and its scene have evolved significantly. Its genres have overlapped and subdivided. In fact, UK trance trailblazer Sasha points out that, confusingly, trance music is now called house, and in his opinion, most DJs do not know what genre they are spinning. Electronic music events have changed, too, becoming large, sanctioned affairs with security and medical personnel. "It's a different culture now," Sasha says. "[In the 1990s,] there was a wild west approach to everything. Parties were illegal. . . . [Now] people are able to party in safe environments."[13] Clearly, EDM has come a long way from teenagers' bedrooms to giant televised festivals and the Grammy Awards stage.

$\mathcal{C}$HAPTER TWO

Dance Music Trendsetters

Industry professionals commonly quip that *everyone* wants to be a DJ, but that is not exactly a joke. Thousands of people consider themselves DJs, even though all they may be doing is selecting songs to play one after another. In such a crowd, it can be difficult for dance music artists to stand out. Moreover, in EDM, where the same tracks and hooks are sampled, almost nothing is new. Yet through creative music making and marketing, some acts manage to rise above the rest.

Daft Punk: Innovative and Timeless

In 2013, Daft Punk's track "Get Lucky" got lucky. Featuring singer Pharrell Williams and legendary guitarist Nile Rodgers, it soared to number one in thirty-four countries and became the best-selling single ever.

Despite their twenty-first-century success, Daft Punk's career had begun twenty years earlier. The group comprises two French DJs named Thomas Bangalter and Guy-Manuel de Homem-Christo, who met in high school in Paris. As teenagers, they played guitar and bass in a rock band and experimented with funk, acid house, and techno. As Daft Punk, they introduced the single "Da Funk" in

1995. Like many songs on their debut album *Homework* (1997), it was what is known as an earworm, a catchy song that people get stuck in their heads. Daft Punk's futuristic sounds and robotic vocals were very danceable—and radically different from the norm. This helped Daft Punk become the first EDM artist ever to be nominated for a Grammy Award. The recognition this brought to electronic music set the stage for Daft Punk to eventually clinch six Grammys by 2014.

One key to Bangalter and Homem-Christo's success is that they are naturally talented and dedicated. Lior Phillips, associate editor of the online magazine *Consequence of Sound*, reviewed *Homework* twenty years after its release. She found it still relevant today, saying, "The two producers were only 22 years old, an incredibly early age given the clarity and grace they had exuded in this complete and timeless masterpiece. In fact, it's become more or less an instruction manual for current would-be producers."[14] Notably, Daft Punk devote considerable time to crafting their songs; they spent several years and more than $1 million composing their 2013 album *Random Access Memories*, for example.

But becoming a big star often requires having more than raw talent. Early on, Daft Punk generated intrigue by wearing robot helmets during their shows, making fans speculate about their identity—a tactic later copied by Deadmau5, Marshmello, and other DJs. Bangalter says of their robot personas, "We're the guys behind the curtains pushing some buttons. We like this idea of stimulating the imagination."[15] In 2001, Daft Punk further marketed themselves by appearing in a Gap commercial at a time when DJs did not appear in ads.

Daft Punk's innovative marketing decisions allowed them to make a living without solely relying on album sales; for example,

"We're the guys behind the curtains pushing some buttons. We like this idea of stimulating the imagination."[15]

—Thomas Bangalter, one of the DJs from Daft Punk

By blending classical music with electronic sounds, Daft Punk (pictured) mastered music completely different from their club hits to make the soundtrack for the movie Tron: Legacy.

the producers were able to license their music to Virgin Records from their own record company, Daft Trax. Thus they maintained control of their music and fortune, a practice that was rare for DJs then. The duo also appeared in ads for Apple's iPod and for Coca Cola and starred in the video game *DJ Hero*. Next they mastered music that was completely different from their club hits, blending classical music with electronic sounds for the soundtrack of the movie *Tron: Legacy* (2010). These accomplishments earned Daft Punk a net worth of $140 million as of 2017.

Daft Punk's most significant achievement was probably its mind-blowing performance at the annual Coachella Music Festival in 2006. So rarely did Daft Punk play at festivals that forty thousand fans flocked to a tent that could hold only ten thousand.

Not only did the duo bang out a set list that many reviewers consider their best ever, but they did it inside a giant lighted pyramid that reportedly cost $300,000 to construct. LED lights were synchronized with the music, and visuals were displayed on a huge screen. "No one had seen anything like that," notes music critic Michaelangelo Matos. "No one had seen that level of production." He recalls attendees texting to their friends, "This is the greatest thing I've ever seen! You're missing the greatest performance of all time."[16] Because of the headlines Daft Punk generated, corporations realized dance music fans had been an untapped festival audience. Soon, Mastercard, T-Mobile, and Disney began sponsoring EDM events, which further popularized the genre.

Today the French DJs known as Daft Punk continue to earn accolades. Two tunes they created with R&B singer The Weeknd in 2016 reached the top five on the *Billboard* 100, proving their success has endured.

Tiësto Keeps Up with Trends

Voted the Greatest DJ of All Time by *Mixmag* in 2011, Tiësto (born Tijs Verwest) started DJing parties at age fourteen in the Netherlands where he grew up. When he was only sixteen, he became a resident DJ at a club. Though Tiësto initially produced hardcore EDM in the 1990s, he soon made a leap to a style almost its opposite: trance. This was in part inspired by Sven Väth, a German trance DJ whom Tiësto praises for discovering great, unknown tracks. Tiësto recalls, "I listened to him for six hours and there was not one single record I recognized." He remembers thinking, "Everything he plays is amazing. . . . That's what I want to do."[17]

True to his word, Tiësto became one of three top trance DJs in the world, according to *Magnetic Magazine*. Above all, the Dutch DJ knows how to stay at the forefront of the EDM scene. He spun a record-breaking twelve-hour solo set in 1999, when it was unheard of for a DJ to perform for that long without the support of any costars or openers. Then, in 2000, Tiësto remixed the song "Silence" by Canadian singer Sarah McLachlan,

Zedd Brings His Classical Background to EDM

The son of two classically trained musicians, the DJ known as Zedd also plays the drums and piano. Born Anton Zaslavski, the German producer was inspired by the DJ duo Justice, who debuted in 2007. Two years later, Zedd began creating dance music and immediately won two remix contests on the EDM site Beatport. Soon after, he composed two singles that occupied number 1 on Beatport's charts for weeks. Then, his reworking of Lady Gaga's "Born This Way" was chosen to appear on the deluxe edition of her album. With each of these accomplishments, he gained respect, fans, and fame.

Zedd's background in classical music composition allows him to create dance tracks that are unusually advanced. According to *Magnetic Magazine*, "Zedd's stellar development is undoubtedly linked to his unique and highly recognizable style of composition. It stands out in a crowded field as meticulously detailed and carefully produced." This made him a good match for the *National Geographic* miniseries *One Strange Rock*, for which he composed a cinematic piano piece.

On *The Late Show with David Letterman* in 2013, Zedd performed "Clarity" (which later won a Grammy) without DJ equipment. Instead, he played an acoustic version on the piano, accompanied by a string quartet and the British singer known as Foxes. Impressively, Zedd earned a Grammy nomination for "Stay" sung by Alessia Cara, while "Break Free" voiced by Ariana Grande hit number four on the *Billboard* 100. Since 2013, Zedd has raked in more than $100 million, proving that his unique talents are appreciated.

Magnetic Magazine, "Zedd Bio," July 1, 2015. www.magneticmag.com.

which introduced her numerous North American pop fans to his talents. Soon he was asked to perform at the 2004 Olympic Games, making him the first DJ ever to do so. Tiësto has also cofounded the label Black Hole Recordings, launched a Guess clothing line, and is a figure in the legendary Madame Tussaud's Wax Museum.

For decades, Tiësto has kept his finger on the pulse of electronic music. As the popularity of trance waned, Tiësto switched to producing house toward the end of the first decade of the

2000s. This kept his music popular with teens. He says, "It's nice to be in touch with the new kids that are coming up—the 16- to 18-year-olds who are producing house music. . . . They see me as kind of a godfather."[18] More recently, Tiësto has broadened his base by working with American producers such as Wolfgang Gartner and Kshmr, as well as stars of other genres, including the indie group Tegan and Sara, singer Nelly Furtado, and rappers Post Malone and Three 6 Mafia.

Tiësto made $33 million in 2018, making him the third-highest-paid DJ on the planet. He generously uses his fame and fortune to help others. The DJ became an ambassador for the charity Dance4Life, which uses club music to raise awareness among young people about HIV/AIDS. Throughout his career, Tiësto has mentored many young artists, including Hardwell, who is from

Tiësto (pictured during a performance in the Netherlands) has used his fame and fortune to raise awareness about HIV/AIDS. He has also mentored many young artists.

Tiësto's hometown. Another of Tiësto's protégés, Martin Garrix, became one of *DJ Mag*'s top 100 DJs as a teen; in 2018 he reached number one on the list and performed at the Winter Olympic Games in South Korea. Martin Garrix says he owes it all to Tiësto, adding, "I can only hope and dream that my performance will inspire others like Tiësto's inspired me."[19]

Annie Mac: Queen of Dance

Hailing from Ireland, Annie McManus was an English literature major who loved underground music by the likes of DJ Sneak and Cajmere. After earning a master's degree in radio, she moved to London. There McManus broke into the music industry despite being an outsider from Ireland and being female in a male-dominated landscape (even as recently as 2018, the world's fifteen richest DJs were male). With a knack for predicting which hopeful musicians would become stars, Annie Mac became a presenter on the modern hits station BBC Radio 1 in 2004. Her *Annie Mac Presents* radio show highlights budding artists, unique sounds, and lesser-known EDM genres. She launched the careers of many new acts, including Disclosure, whose remix she featured on her *Annie Mac Presents 2012* compilation album. Soon after, Disclosure's debut album was nominated for a coveted Mercury Prize in the UK, as well as a Grammy in America.

> "*Annie Mac Presents* [is] . . . making Annie herself one of the most in-demand club/festival DJs."[20]
>
> —*Mixmag* dance music magazine

As Annie Mac's show was gaining notice, she was also becoming a respected club DJ. Rather than focus on one genre, her sets combine dubstep, house, drum and bass, and more. As *Mixmag* has noted, "*Annie Mac Presents* [is] constantly providing a platform for a generation of youthful, bass-driven, live dance acts and making Annie herself one of the most in-demand club/festival DJs on the planet."[20]

Dubbed the "Queen of Dance," Annie Mac won the Best Female award at the 2009 Drum and Bass Awards. She continues to tour, holding down the mainstage in massive clubs worldwide, including in Ibiza. Her radio career has flourished, too. In 2015 she began hosting another popular show on weeknights on Radio 1. Meanwhile, her Friday night dance show captures more than a million radio listeners. Annie Mac also founded the annual Lost & Found Festival on the Mediterranean island of Malta, which brings in thousands of tourists and has earned her the title "Festival Ambassador of Malta." She also developed AMP Sounds, a monthlong event that features nine different concerts across England. In addition, Annie Mac's documentary on UK club culture, *Who Killed the Night?*, aired in 2017, and the following year she hosted the Mercury Music Awards show.

Annie Mac has helped pave the way for women in EDM. Though it was not easy at first, she has stood up for herself when she experienced sexism—for example, pushing back when show promoters featured scantily dressed go-go dancers during her sets. "I've been in excruciating situations, DJing surrounded by half-naked women on podiums," she says. "It took me years to pluck up the courage to tell promoters that I didn't like the message it gave out."[21]

Today Annie Mac uses her influence to support women's issues. Consider that music promoters book mostly male DJs; for example, *HuffPost* reporter Alanna Vagianos points out that in 2016, the Ultra Music Festival in Miami, which is an all-electronic music gathering, booked ten times as many male performers as female ones—there were just 20 female acts, compared to 198 all-male acts. In response, Annie Mac made the groundbreaking decision to feature in her 2019 Lost & Found Festival a 50 percent female lineup, which included esteemed artists Peggy Gou and the Black Madonna. The music writer known simply as androids sums up Annie Mac's influence this way: "She's so important, she's literally nurturing the next wave of bass music youth."[22]

David Guetta: King of Pop-EDM

The eighth-highest-paid DJ in the world is Pierre David Guetta, who uses only his middle and last names professionally. David Guetta holds club residencies, sells branded luxury items, owns a twenty-four-hour club in the Ibiza airport, and produces hits with the world's biggest stars. Beginning in the 1980s, he played house and hip-hop across his home country of France. Early on he learned to command attention during shows instead of hiding behind the decks.

Guetta gained an international audience by working with non-French artists; for example, he featured American singer Chris Willis on several tracks and remixed a song by British rocker David Bowie. In 2009 he collaborated with the US hip-hop/pop group the Black-Eyed Peas for their single, "I Gotta Feeling," which catapulted him to pop chart glory. Downloaded 9 million times, "I Gotta Feeling" holds a US record for downloads on iTunes. Two years later, Guetta again struck gold with "Titanium," featuring then-unknown Australian singer Sia. The track reached number seven on *Billboard*'s Hot 100 and, according to Nielsen Sound-Scan, had sold nearly 4 million copies by 2014. Guetta also has earned recognition by winning multiple awards, including two Grammys.

Part of what makes Guetta stand out is his savvy branding. His company, which he launched in 1996, sells items such as luggage tags, sunglasses, and bikinis that are geared toward trendy jetsetters. Guetta has also endorsed products for other companies, such as Beats headphones and special edition TAG Heuer watches. From these business ventures and his DJ sets, he made $15 million in 2018.

Now in his fifties, Guetta has managed to stay relevant with young fans, partly because he has successfully crossed over into pop, hip-hop, and R&B. For instance, his song "Where Them Girls At" features hip-hop artists Flo Rida and Nicki Minaj, and he has worked with rappers Lil Wayne and Kid Cudi, as well as pop and R&B singers Usher, Rihanna, and Jennifer Hudson. Another way he keeps fans engaged is by incorporating props and live acts in his sets, such as burlesque dancers, trapeze acts, and glitter cannons; once, his show featured a woman who rode a horse onto the dance floor.

After more than three decades in the EDM industry, Guetta has not only racked up an astounding 52 million Facebook fans but has changed the face of pop music. "You can hear his fingerprints all over tons of other artists' work," notes *Rolling Stone*, adding, "Whenever a Top 40 star starts singing a feel-good hook over a house pulse, they should probably consider cutting this guy a check."[23]

David Guetta performs at a festival in 2016. Guetta has not only racked up an astounding 52 million Facebook fans but has also changed the face of pop music.

Skrillex Brings Dubstep to the Mainstream

With one side of his head shaved, and long black hair on the other, Sonny Moore, more popularly known as Skrillex, looks more like he belongs in an emo or goth band than in a DJ booth at expensive clubs. Raised in California, Skrillex is, in fact, a singer in an emo band. He decided he wanted to be a DJ after visiting a Utah record store where an employee introduced him to classic drum and bass records. "He played 2 for me that I ended up buying that day: DJ Baron 'Operation Pipe Dream' & Pendulum 'Hold Your Color,'" Skrillex later tweeted. "I had already loved electronic music but after that day I told myself I would be a DJ."[24]

Nervo, the Highest-Paid Female DJs

The EDM group Nervo comprises twin sisters Olivia and Miriam Nervo, who began their music career around 2000, when they landed a deal to write songs for pop stars and EDM artists. It was David Guetta who convinced the sisters to learn to DJ. A decade later, they were generating hits with Grammy-winning producer Afrojack, pop star Britney Spears, and singer Kylie Minogue. By 2012 Nervo were performing at the prestigious UK dance music festival Creamfields.

As of 2018, no woman had made it onto the *Forbes* top-earning DJs list. But Nervo have come close, earning $9 million from 2013 to 2014, and $10 million from 2015 to 2016 (all the male acts on the list made more). Nervo's fortune comes from spinning more than two hundred sets in some years, holding down residencies in Las Vegas and Ibiza, producing music, and modeling for CoverGirl makeup. They also launched their own record label called Got Me Baby! Records.

All their hard work has paid off more than just financially. Nervo won a Grammy for cowriting David Guetta's tune "When Love Takes Over" (2009). Incredibly, their set at the World Dance Music Radio Awards in 2017 drew a radio audience of more than 10 million listeners, and in 2018 Nervo were honored as the best female mainstream artist at the International Dance Music Awards in Miami.

By 2008 Skrillex was composing electronic music while living on fellow producer 12th Planet's couch in Los Angeles. With raw, hard-hitting, bass-blasting sounds, Skrillex's musical style is sometimes called brostep, a somewhat disparaging term that suggests it appeals only to young white males. But when he gave away his first EP on Myspace (an early social media site), his music gained many fans of all races and genders. He was signed to Deadmau5's label in 2010, and two years later was nominated for five Grammy Awards. "This is really crazy for me, man," said Skrillex when accepting his first of three awards, for his remix of "Cinema" by Benny Benassi. "A year and a half ago, I was making this song in my bedroom—I was actually living in an illegal warehouse space in downtown L.A."[25] Now with eight Grammys under his belt, he holds the world record for Grammys earned by an EDM act.

Skrillex showed his range by creating robotic sounds as a sound designer for the action flick *Transformers: Age of Extinction* (2014), while his earworm "Bangarang" wove its way into the movie *Deadpool 2* (2018). He has worked with the metal band Korn, electro-house duo Knife Party, the band Incubus, and singer Bruno Mars. Skrillex teamed up with fellow EDM kingpin Diplo to produce Justin Bieber's track "Where Are Ü Now," which is credited with revitalizing the pop singer's career. Diplo says of Skrillex, "He was one of my most influential people. . . . He's probably the best of all the DJ artists. He's gone as far as anybody, had the most cultural impact as anybody."[26]

"[Skrillex is] probably the best of all the DJ artists. He's gone as far as anybody, had the most cultural impact as anybody."[26]

—Diplo, a DJ and record label owner

Much of Skrillex's success is due to his genius for marketing. An avid gamer, he creatively released his 2014 album *Recess* through a phone app video game called *Alien Ride*. As users played, they unlocked access to the album's unreleased songs. The tracks were available only briefly, and players were given a link to preorder the album on iTunes.

Skrillex also helps new DJs make a name for themselves. In 2010, a young producer now known as Zedd sent Skrillex a track of his music, which is influenced by a range of genres from metal to classical. Skrillex liked the track so much that he played it in his set that night and later that year signed Zedd to his record label, OWSLA. Zedd has since become a Grammy-winning superstar. Skrillex also shares, via social media, his favorite singles by budding artists. This brought fame to Marshmello, who produces future bass and made $21 million only two years later, in 2017. Skrillex himself earns an estimated $200,000 per performance and is a multimillionaire, having leveraged his unusual style into a lucrative career.

While these influential DJs have shaped EDM, many others, from Kaskade to Calvin Harris to Avicii, have made their mark on the industry, too. Even though they spend their time behind the decks, unable to run across the stage amping up the audience like rockers do, these master DJs draw colossal crowds to their sets.

CHAPTER THREE

Building a Fan Base

Forest Green, a San Francisco DJ, spends 80 percent of her time promoting her shows but only 20 percent creating music. This is because DJs make the bulk of their income from shows, not song or album sales. Consider that fans can buy Calvin Harris's albums for about $10 each, but, according to *Forbes*, his sets in Las Vegas bring him roughly $500,000 apiece; festivals, meanwhile, may pay him $1 million. To attract fans to money-making events like festivals and shows, DJs use music sharing sites, streaming services, and social media to publicize not just their music but their own personal identity, too. Developing a brand that embodies their personality is how they gain loyal followers.

With the rise of music distribution websites and social networking, EDM artists can rack up fans without needing to rely on a record label. DJs often do this via a combination of music sites and applications. SoundCloud, Spotify, and Apple Music have the most listeners, but sites like Mixcloud or Beatport are useful, too. Which service producers use depends on what features they value, whether they can afford to pay for premium or membership-based services, and whether they want to receive small stipends, called royalties, for each play. Newer artists are usually willing to give away songs to entice people to listen, while more established ones might offer tracks as paid downloads only.

SoundCloud Is Suited for Self-Promotion

As the largest audio platform in the world, SoundCloud handles music streaming and distribution. With 76 million monthly US listeners, it features remixes, mash-ups, and obscure tracks. DJs can upload two hours' worth of music for free; after that they can pay for a subscription, such as SoundCloud Pro, to get access to additional features.

Kygo (Kyrre Gørvell-Dahll), a young Norwegian DJ, is an excellent example of someone who has used SoundCloud to promote his music. Amazingly, he taught himself how to produce tracks and DJ solely by watching YouTube tutorials. Then, each

As the largest audio platform in the world, SoundCloud handles both music streaming and distribution. DJs can upload two hours' worth of music to the platform for free.

month, he uploaded one remix to SoundCloud and shared it through his Facebook page. A year later, Kygo had tens of thousands of followers. In 2013, at age twenty-three, he attracted international attention by reworking pop singer Ed Sheeran's song, "I See Fire." Kygo's remix has nearly 70 million plays on SoundCloud, and Sheeran said he liked it almost as much as the original. Record companies began courting Kygo, and he signed with Sony/ATV in 2015. As he finished his first album, *Cloud Nine*, he posted preview tracks on SoundCloud to encourage preorder sales.

With 1.5 million SoundCloud followers as of 2019, Kygo is a testament to how the platform can be used to launch a person's career. His popularity on SoundCloud helped him break a record on Spotify, a different music platform, where his songs were streamed a billion times in just one year (2015). He also made history in 2015 when he became the first EDM artist to play at the Nobel Peace Prize ceremony in Norway and less than a year later became the first house DJ to spin at the Olympic Games.

How Streaming Sites Pull In Fans and Money

The British streaming site Mixcloud is much smaller than Sound-Cloud but offers DJs a different audience and, potentially, more royalties. Mixcloud is a hub for podcasts, live sets, and 15 million radio shows. Through Mixcloud, listeners can discover EDM acts from around the world. Although the site is free, users can pay to subscribe to certain DJs' channels to access more music. After fees are paid to record labels and original artists whose tracks a DJ has sampled, the DJ keeps more than half of the revenue, which is a significant amount. The DJ known as Eats Everything predicts that this service will help artists collect fans and an income, too. "People are putting hours, days, weeks, even months into making music, and they're not getting paid," he says. "I do OK touring, but there are a lot of artists who don't, and this will be the first time they're making anything from music."[27]

Some DJs gain fans by getting their tunes showcased on the two major streaming sites, Spotify and Apple Music. The world's most widely used streaming platform, Spotify, has 175 million users. Incredibly, these users stream EDM songs 12 billion times per month, according to a 2017 International Music Summit report. The second-largest site, Apple Music, has 50 million subscribers. Both sites offer music playlists geared toward EDM fans. If a song lands on a popular playlist, the potential audience for the song is massive.

Some artists complain that neither Apple Music nor Spotify pay musicians enough for their work. Indeed, artists earn less than a penny for each stream—and that is for a full song. If only part of a track is sampled, the DJ gets a fraction of that. Regardless, *FACT Magazine* writer Scott Wilson suggests that DJs put their music on streaming sites more for the publicity. In Wilson's opinion, "the royalties may not add up to much, but the benefits of getting featured on a platform like Apple Music shouldn't be underestimated. . . . The profile boost alone would make up for the relative lack of royalties."[28]

The Power of Social Media

Given the sheer amount of EDM available on streaming sites, producers must work hard to make themselves and their music memorable. Rebekah Farrugia, associate professor of media studies at Oakland University in Michigan, contends that "having a recognizable brand helps DJs stand out from their competition, which in an increasingly hyper-competitive DJ market has become more and more important."[29] DJs' brands encompass not just their musical style but also their image, the way they talk, and what they speak out about. Generally, dance music artists advertise their brand through their social media accounts. Promoting events on social networks is key because EDM fans

"Having a recognizable brand helps DJs stand out from their competition."[29]

—Rebekah Farrugia, associate professor of media studies

DJs Link Up with Clubs to Gain Fans

Clubbing is big business—in 2018, nightclub events, or "club nights," that featured EDM brought in $965 million. This has happened in part because entrepreneurial DJs have teamed up with clubs. In 1994, for example, progressive house pioneers Sasha and John Digweed changed the way DJs marketed themselves. At the time, DJs who held residencies at nightclubs occasionally recorded their mixes and handed out the mixtapes to advertise their club night. Sasha and Digweed went further, though, by working with one of England's biggest clubs, Renaissance, to create the first album professionally produced and marketed by a nightclub. Released on the club's own record label, the three-disc *Renaissance: The Mix Collection* promoted Sasha and Digweed's residencies there and created an even bigger audience for their music. Their mix was, as the EDM online magazine *Resident Advisor* calls it, "the great Daddy of all DJ mix compilations—the cornerstone for all things progressive, and a massive influence for legions of DJs to follow."

Sasha and Digweed's album was the first of many that promoted DJs' club sets. Renaissance continued to produce mix compilations by artists such as Deep Dish, Danny Howells, and Roger Sanchez. London's famous club Fabric, a giant 25,000-square-foot (2323 sq. m) space, also got in on the act. Over seventeen years, it released two hundred CDs, each of which showcased a talented DJ such as Diplo, Flava D, Ricardo Villalobos, Cassy, Claude VonStroke, and Nina Kraviz. The releases gave the artists access to the club's fans, and the artists brought crowds into the clubs. Though Sasha and Digweed could not have predicted how massive the club industry would become, their partnership with it formed a blueprint that is still followed today.

Resident Advisor, "10 Years On—Paul Oakenfold's Goa Mix Still Sounds Fresh," February 4, 2005. www.residentadvisor.net.

often buy concert and festival tickets through links shared on social networks. According to the ticket seller Ticketfly, social media platforms drive six times more ticket sales for EDM events than for any other type of concert, sporting event, or theater production.

The social media site YouTube can be an abundant source of fans; for example, Skrillex's YouTube channel has 5 billion views and 18 million subscribers. It is much more difficult for artists to earn money on this platform, however. That's because YouTube is the lowest paying of the major music sites. Since each play earns an artist only $0.00069, artists need a *lot* of clicks to earn a meaningful amount of money. To increase their visibility, some artists post not just their own music but also tutorials on how to DJ. The Dutch producer Laidback Luke, for example, uses his YouTube channel to dispense DJing advice, review other artists' music, share behind-the-scenes tour videos, and call out his favorite social media comments from fans, which encourages user interaction. His interviews with more-famous DJs, such as Afrojack, help drive new fans to his channel, which now has about 20 million views.

Some EDM artists use humor to capture new viewers; for example, Dillon Francis, who produces moombahton and electro house music, promotes himself through his YouTube series "One Deep Talks." Portraying a clueless German called DJ Hanzel, he interviews giants of EDM, such as Alesso, Anna Lunoe, and Flosstradamus. In

Dillon Francis (pictured) uses YouTube regularly to promote his brand. One YouTube favorite is his "Get Low" music video, which has a staggering 558 million views.

another video on his channel, Francis answers Twitter users' DJing questions in his own snarky style. One YouTube favorite is his silly "Get Low" music video with DJ Snake, which has a staggering 558 million views. Another video follows up on a contest Francis ran on Twitter and Instagram in which he promised to wax his friend Zedd's name into his own chest hair. It depicts the DJ's painful experience, with Zedd holding his hand. By filming comedic activities that are part of his unusual lifestyle, Francis provides his 2 million YouTube subscribers an inside look into his mind as well as his music.

Instagram, which has a billion monthly users, is another source of fans. Although users are limited to sharing photos and sixty-second videos, some EDM artists have mastered a formula for gaining followers. Russian producer Nina Kraviz, for example, was listed in *DJ Mag*'s top six DJs to follow on Instagram. With a million followers, her account displays photos of her homeland (Siberia), as well as photos of her travels, album art, clips from live shows, photos of herself with other DJs, and a segment of her lecture at Red Bull Music Academy. Fans pay attention to these posts: A picture of Kraviz stamping vinyl records with her logo, for example, received more than thirteen thousand likes. Another Instagram tactic some DJs use is to post screen-shots of themselves chatting with industry bigwigs, which makes fans feel privy to insider conversations.

These artists all use social media to share their personalities with the world, and fans flock to their accounts even if what they say is controversial. Deadmau5, for instance, is an outspoken critic of other artists. On social media, he has insulted DJs such as Marshmello, Porter Robinson, Afrojack, and Hardwell. This habit makes him respected by some and at least talked about by others. His strategy has worked; he has 8.5 million fans on Facebook and landed on the cover of a *Rolling Stone* issue in which he dissed several musicians, including Madonna.

On the opposite side of the spectrum is Kaskade, who frequently praises other producers and whose song "Room for Happiness" is so inspiring that several fans have the chorus tattooed on their bodies. "People know my lyrics," he says, "and it's all about life, love, happiness and these big euphoric moments."[30] Tickets to Kaskade's shows are often priced lower than other EDM artists' because he wants them to be affordable for fans. Kaskade is further set apart by being a practicing Mormon who does not drink or get high. He is also ranked number four on *Rolling Stone*'s list of DJs who rule the world. It seems that for nearly all EDM acts, there are countless potential fans waiting to connect with them.

Marshmello's Virtual Concert Captures New Fans

Beyond the usual music sites, some EDM acts are finding more creative avenues to tap into new audiences. Consider how Marshmello (Chris Comstock) used the video game *Fortnite* to promote himself. *Fortnite* is so popular with young people that, according to the analytics agency Newzoo, 68 percent of gamers between ten and thirty years old play it.

With this in mind, on February 18, 2019, Marshmello played a live concert within *Fortnite* that drew the largest audience of any virtual concert in history. Nearly 11 million people stopped playing the game for ten minutes while Marshmello DJed a motion-captured performance on a virtual stage complete with strobe lights, costumed go-go dancers, and impressive visuals. The concert was also integrated into players' gaming experience; for example, when he dropped the track "I Can Fly," players' avatars suddenly gained the ability to float in the air.

Because virtual concerts take place via technology, they have the ability to reach listeners of all ages, backgrounds, income levels, and geographical areas. Recognizing that many of his *Fortnite* concertgoers were minors, Marshmello tweeted, "What makes me happiest about today is that so many people got to experience their first concert ever."[31] More than that, they be-

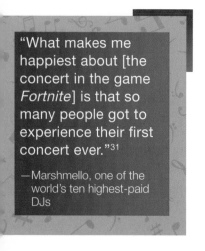

"What makes me happiest about [the concert in the game *Fortnite*] is that so many people got to experience their first concert ever."[31]

—Marshmello, one of the world's ten highest-paid DJs

Beatport Helps DJs Launch Their Careers

Beatport is a digital music store where DJs can legally buy and sell electronic music; that is, they can remix other artists' songs and sell them without violating copyright law. The more a producer's tracks are purchased, the more visibility they get on Beatport, and the more fans they acquire.

The British duo CamelPhat are a prime example of how this works. CamelPhat's tunes "Cola" and "Hangin' Out with Charlie" were featured on Beatport's monthly Best New Tracks list, after which their number of downloads skyrocketed. Both songs made a clean sweep of Beatport's top tracks of 2017, taking the number one and two spots. This earned CamelPhat the additional honor of being Beatport's artist of the year. Since then, they have collected 158,000 Instagram followers, were featured on the popular *Essential Mix* radio show hosted by Pete Tong, and have spun at the UK's Creamfields festival.

Hardwell is another producer whose fame was boosted by Beatport. In 2011 his track with Tiësto, "Zero 76," soared to number one on Beatport, and his track "Cobra" made the site's Top 10 list. Then, Hardwell had an incredible seven consecutive number one hits on Beatport. By 2013, at age twenty-five, he had acquired enough fans to be ranked the number one DJ by readers of *DJ Mag*, mostly due to the publicity generated on Beatport.

came instant fans. In the days following the virtual *Fortnite* concert, Marshmello had 699,000 new subscribers to his YouTube channel, 62,000 new followers on Twitter, and almost 260,000 new followers on Instagram. He also gained 5,200 followers on Twitch, the video-streaming platform on which his *Fortnite* concert was live-streamed. Generally, gaining new followers translates to increased ticket sales; in fact, the ticket seller Songkick noted that more visitors searched its site for Marshmello tickets in the four days after the virtual concert than they had over the previous three months altogether. Given this success, more EDM acts will likely target gamers using embedded virtual concerts.

Harnessing Star Power

DJs also earn fans by collaborating with other popular musicians, a strategy that has been employed since the 1990s when the pop group U2 took DJ Paul Oakenfold on tour as its opening act to get fans dancing at U2 shows. More recently, DJs have produced tracks by bands that already have large followings; for example, Noisia and Excision have produced multiple tracks with the band Korn; Deadmau5 has collaborated with Foo Fighters; and Avicii has created multiple hits with the band Coldplay. Similarly, the Scottish DJ known as Calvin Harris became a house-

The Weeknd has released EDM-influenced tracks, and helped accelerate the career of the DJ duo Snakehips.

hold name when he wrote and produced Rihanna's hit "We Found Love." Their electro house single spent ten weeks at number one on the *Billboard* Hot 100, longer than any other song that year (2011). Since then, Calvin Harris has amassed about 16 million subscribers on YouTube and is the world's highest-paid DJ.

Another way DJs grow their fan base is by sampling or remixing songs by other musicians. This has been the strategy of Snakehips, a DJ duo from Britain. They have reworked songs by the band Wild Belle, the EDM duo Bondax, and the trip hop/alternative singer Banks. But they struck gold when they remixed the song "Wanderlust," originally by the pop sensation known as the Weeknd. The Weeknd tweeted about the remix to his millions of followers, leading it to be played more than 1.5 million times in less than a month. Meanwhile, Snakehips got recognition for their own grooves as well; their first song on SoundCloud, "On and On," has been played nearly 2 million times since 2013, and the DJs now perform around the world.

DJs also build fans by entering remix or production contests. As the name implies, contestants either remix or produce a song. Usually, anyone can enter regardless of age or skill level. Winners get prizes, mentoring from industry professionals, and, most importantly, name recognition. Consider one international remix contest launched by Afrojack in 2018. The five winning tracks were featured on an EP released on Afrojack's own label, Wall Recordings, bringing previously unheard artists much exposure. "I like helping people," says Afrojack. "It's so easy for me with the network I've built over the years to introduce cool new people to long established big names. That really excites me, that I can sort of recycle my network. . . . I can actually supply it to others."[32] Indeed, he helped jumpstart the careers of admired

> "I like helping people. . . . It's so easy for me with the network I've built over the years to introduce cool new [DJs] to long established big names."[32]
>
> —Afrojack, Grammy-winning producer

stars R3hab and Quintino, as well as a DJ from Los Angeles called Vice.

Newer artists can acquire fans by getting a big name in EDM to play or remix their own tracks. Once the star's mix gets publicized, listeners are likely to discover the original artist. Fans can see this strategy at work on Hardwell's weekly radio show, *Hardwell on Air*, when he plays the Demo of the Week that is sent to him by a hopeful DJ. His 50 million listeners get introduced to emerging artists, who have included Kristianex & Taabz and the Finnish group Winning Team. Playing new music also gives a boost to more-established DJs, as discovering new artists or underground tracks is a respected skill. Jace Clayton, known as DJ Rupture, says, "Enterprising DJs can make money and a name for them-selves by being the middlemen between the source of the hot new track and its potential audience."[33] In this sense, playing or remixing other artists' tracks benefits both parties.

Chart-Toppers Earn Fans

The two New Yorkers who formed the Chainsmokers make songs that lend themselves to remixing, but that is not the only method they use to increase their popularity. The Chainsmok-ers have mastered a formula for earning the respect and loy-alty of millions of fans. First, they produce tracks aimed at the pop charts, because pop is mainstream and has more fans than electronic music. Typically, artists on the pop singles charts have completed an album, and they release one single at a time to promote album sales. But Charlie Harding, a songwriter who cohosts the *Switched on Pop* podcast, notes that the Chain-smokers took a different approach. Without creating an album, they pumped out one hit after another through 2015 and 2016. According to Harding, "They just keep producing these singles and trying to place them one after another on the charts. I don't think anyone's doing that."[34] In this way, the duo became fa-mous by continuously topping the charts. Then, when the

Chainsmokers released their first album in 2017, they cleverly boosted it to number one on the *Billboard* 200 by including the album when fans bought tickets to their shows. Now they have 8.6 million likes on Facebook and are the highest-paid American DJs, earning $45.5 million in 2018.

Through creative self-promotion, EDM artists attract the attention of fans—and more-popular DJs who might help them propel their career. "Artists will need to put their marketing hats on, brush up on their social media skills and . . . get out of their studios,"[35] says producer Dan Larson, also known as Middle Child. As Larson suggests, prosperous artists excel by aggressively marketing their own unique brand both online and in person.

CHAPTER FOUR

EDM Is Here to Stay

With the global EDM industry valued at $7.3 billion in 2018, it is too profitable to fade away. Indeed, electronic music is cemented in daily life—one can hear it on TV show soundtracks, in retail stores, and in elevators in countries all over the world. It has permeated music genres ranging from country to metal. Not only that, exciting developments are predicted for the future. Dance music festivals are growing; in 2018 alone, 160 million tickets were sold, up from 147 million the year before. To create engaging shows, producers are tinkering with wild new sounds and designing awe-inspiring effects. Furthermore, by starting their own record companies and products, DJs ensure that their names and unique styles will be recognized for years to come.

EDM Has Influenced Nearly All Genres

Forward-thinking EDM artists borrow sounds from many different genres and in the process are changing the sound of most other music. Rida Naser, a host on the SiriusXM dance channel BPM, predicts, "We've been seeing major collaborations between all kinds of genres, but . . . those will evolve into something bigger than ever. Hitting different audiences in different genres will be the key. You'll see dance music/ artists reach into places you'd least expect!"[36]

One example of this is hard rock and metal. Bassnectar, a death metal band member who became a festival DJ, made his mark by remixing tracks by White Zombie, Nine Inch Nails, and Sepulveda. Bands like Korn and Linkin Park have added electronic music to their songs. In fact, as recently as the first decade of the 2000s, electronic music birthed the subgenre of electronicore, which fuses EDM with metal and hardcore punk; nu-disco, an EDM-disco blend; and moombahton, which is house- and reggae-inspired.

Bassnectar performs at a festival in 2015. The former death metal band member made his mark as a festival DJ by remixing hard rock music tracks from bands like Nine Inch Nails and White Zombie.

Few people dreamed that EDM's influence would spread to country music. Yet Swedish producer Avicii stunned the crowd at the EDM-only Ultra Music Festival in 2013 when he did just that. Alongside a bluegrass band playing banjos and a kazoo, he debuted his folk-influenced song "Wake Me Up." Though it received some boos from dance music purists in attendance, it ultimately became a hit, and Avicii was credited with popularizing the new genre of folktronica. Some country artists who have jumped on

Steve Aoki's Global Empire

Steven Aoki, who is of Japanese descent, is the only Asian artist on the *Forbes* list of highest-paid DJs. Hailing from California, he has cemented EDM's staying power by propping up new producers and plastering his electro house grooves all over movies, TV, and even casinos, where gambling machines feature his tracks.

As a teen, Aoki started Dim Mak Records with only $400. Notably, he ran the company from his college dorm room for years before he became a celebrity; in contrast, most DJs start labels *after* they have found fame and fortune. "I'm holding a mirror, so when attention comes towards me, I'm pointing the mirror towards artists I think are the next young guns and pioneers of sound," he explains. To rev up crowds, Aoki engages in stage antics, such as crowdsurfing across the audience in a blowup life raft. He has worked with countless stars, including Linkin Park, Nervo, Lauren Jauregui (their "One Kiss" won best dance song at the 2018 Teen Choice Awards), and even blockbuster filmmaker J.J. Abrams. And with a bachelor's degree in feminist studies, he claims to fight gender discrimination wherever he sees it in the industry.

Music is not Aoki's only business venture. He has appeared on TV shows such as his own *Aoki's World*, had a cameo in the movie *Why Him?* (2016), and is in the Grammy-nominated documentary *I'll Sleep When I'm Dead*. The DJ also appears in video games, one of which features ten of his own tracks. Finally, Aoki puts out a clothing line, creates Aoki Bootcamp fitness videos, and manages the Steve Aoki Charitable Fund for global humanitarian causes.

Zack O'Malley Greenburg, "From Skrillex to Steve Aoki: Inside the Rise of DJ-Owned Labels," *Forbes*, August 24, 2015. www.forbes.com.

the EDM bandwagon include singer Maren Morris, who lent vocals to the number one single "The Middle" with Zedd and Grey; Florida Georgia Line, which was featured on two dance tracks in 2017; and the Zac Brown Band, which released an EDM-heavy hit. Even Taylor Swift, who began as a country singer, has put out an electro-pop album (*Reputation*) with hints of house, dubstep, and trap. With each endeavor, electronic music becomes increasingly accepted by country music fans, who in 2018 numbered more than 115 million.

Tapping into an even bigger audience, EDM is melding with rap and hip-hop, a genre which in 2017 surpassed rock music as the most popular in the United States. DJs Nick Catchdubs and A-Trak were ahead of the curve in this area; they incorporate hip-hop and EDM into their sets and started Fool's Gold Records in 2007 to promote artists of both genres. Their label released tunes by Kid Cudi and Kid Sister, both rappers who dabble in electronic music sounds, as well as the trap act Flosstradamus, among others. Fans appreciate the signature sound of Fool's Gold Records, which has 8 million followers on SoundCloud—more than most EDM labels.

Even more surprising than the rap-EDM partnership is club music's crossover with classical music and jazz. Several innovators have dipped into these genres. Consider the revolutionary *New Forms* (1997) by UK artists Roni Size and Reprazent. This drum and bass album incorporated a French horn, violin, bass viol, and acoustic guitar. It even won a Mercury Prize, the UK's highest honor for an album. Today, the mixing of these genres has resulted in symphony orchestras playing instrumental versions of dance tracks. In Europe, for example, orchestras cover classic electronic tracks by Jeff Mills, Basement Jaxx, Goldie, Faithless, and BT.

In 2018, a jazz album unexpectedly put out by Borgore, an EDM producer and rapper from Israel, also pushed musical boundaries. Borgore was famous for his profane, egotistical lyrics and hard-hitting dubstep. "Borgore and jazz go together like peanut butter and toothpaste," writes Matthew Meadow, editor in chief of YourEDM. "It just doesn't really make sense."[37] Unfazed, however, Borgore promoted his shows by playing with a jazz band, and he himself is trained in piano, saxophone, and drums. His jazz version of his dubstep track "Decisions" (originally recorded with Miley Cyrus) had the audience raucously singing along. By merging with a different genre, DJs gain respect while taking electronic music in a new direction.

The Future of EDM Festivals

One challenge for EDM artists is to make their shows interesting even if they play the same set list each night. To outdo each other, DJs put on elaborate stage productions that feature programmed laser lights, fire effects, and short films. On Skrillex's first tour, for example, his custom-built stage was connected to a motion-capture suit he was wearing. Giant avatars behind him mimicked his movements as he DJed.

Creating an engaging show is especially important at festivals, where artists compete with multiple headliners playing on different stages at the same time. Calvin Harris, who so far has the most number one hits in the decade of the 2010s, broke another record in 2016 when he became the first DJ to serve as the main headliner at the giant Coachella Music Festival, with bands and rappers billed below him. His set featured a massive light show, fireworks, and cameo appearances from surprise guests, including Rihanna. His headlining show also demonstrated that even music festivals that have historically featured rock bands are now showcasing DJs as the stars.

The sound at festivals is changing, too. Corporate festival sponsors often want DJs to play "big-tent" mainstream music, which is currently pop-driven electro house and future bass. This makes it difficult for acts who produce less-trendy styles to get booked; however, savvy artists are finding ways to meet the needs of sponsors while also pleasing their underground-music–loving fans. One is producer Mija from Phoenix, Arizona. Music writer Ezra Marcus explains that Mija strikes a balance "by incorporating weirder sounds inspired by the glory days of rave, without sacrificing the horsepower needed to move modern big-tent crowds."[38] In this way, DJs are adjusting their sound to accommodate festivals' changing soundscapes.

Addiction and Depression Are Common in the EDM Scene

Unfortunately, electronic music's rapid growth has put massive pressure on artists. Disturbingly, substance abuse is more common in EDM than in any other music genre, and depression and suicides linked to addiction often occur among DJs.

Fans are also affected: When Drugabuse.com surveyed 976 concertgoers, it found that those attending EDM events were more likely to use drugs or alcohol than were fans of other music genres. Nearly 70 percent of people surveyed at electronic music festivals said they were intoxicated: 55 percent of the concertgoers had consumed alcohol, 29 percent had smoked marijuana, and 26 percent had used ecstasy. In contrast, less than half of those polled at country, R&B, and pop concerts were under the influence.

Among DJs, too, substance abuse is problematic. Tim Bergling, known as Avicii, was hospitalized in 2012 due to binge drinking; the next year, he announced that he was sober. Tragically, in 2018, at age twenty-eight, he committed suicide after he apparently relapsed. This was the same fate of Keith Flint, lead singer of the Prodigy, who committed suicide in 2019 after battling depression and drug addiction. Years earlier, DJ AM in New York and DJ Rashad in Chicago died of drug overdoses.

When music professionals were asked in 2018 what they thought was in store for the EDM industry, several responded that DJs will become more likely to take extended breaks to rejuvenate their mental health. "Artists are going to start to realize the importance of mental health," says Chris Varvaro, a producer who lives in New Jersey. "Living the glamorous life style portrayed on social [media] is not always the case; in fact, it's . . . quite stressful behind the scenes. I really hope people do realize this and take time to be mentally healthy!"

Quoted in Stevo Jacobs, "24 Music Industry Predictions for 2019," EDM Sauce, December 14, 2018. www.edmsauce.com.

Independence

Using their vast connections and wealth, a few artists are producing festivals themselves, without the help of major corporate sponsors. Bassnectar is an example of an American producer who throws multiday festivals where he headlines with supporting acts he has personally vetted. His 2019 DejaVoom event in Cancun, Mexico, offered yoga, painting, a surfing contest, custom merchandise, a pool party with the electronic band Beats Antique, and about thirty other artists. Despite its high-priced tickets, the event sold out, demonstrating fans' willingness to support DJs' more intimate gatherings with a few thousand—rather than hundreds of thousands—of guests.

In a similar trend, EDM artists are more often shunning record labels. Such companies used to be necessary to fund music production and promotion and to put on concerts; yet due to services like TuneCore or CDBaby, through which artists can directly sell their music, more acts are likely to release albums themselves, according to record label executive Mike Darlington. One such story comes from "dubstep violinist" Lindsey Stirling, who plays violin while dancing to dubstep and hip-hop beats. Unable to get her unusual act signed to a label, she started a YouTube channel to showcase her videos. With a growing base of preteens (which is unusual for classical music *or* EDM), she has racked up 11.5 million subscribers on YouTube—even more than Cardi B or Justin Timberlake. In 2015 she became the fourth-highest-paid YouTube star in the world, making $6 million that year from video views.

With that money, Stirling was able to sponsor her own tours and release her own albums. Amazingly, her four albums reached the top twenty-five of the *Billboard* 200; *Shatter Me* (2014) peaked at number two. "If you need someone to motivate you, and if you're not self-driven and if you're not full of ideas all the time, a label's probably a good route," says Stirling. "But if you're someone who's constantly bursting with ideas and loves to just go and doesn't want to wait for [approval from] someone else . . . I think a label would drive me crazy and I'd feel held back."[39] Because Stirling did it on her own, she does not have to share her profits or compromise her art with a record company.

Lindsey Stirling, who plays the violin while dancing to dubstep beats, performs in 2015. Initially unable to get her unusual act signed to a label, she started a YouTube channel to showcase her videos.

EDM Brands Keep Dance Music Alive

Many giants of EDM have launched record companies to ensure that new artists and styles thrive. Label owners include Calvin Harris, Above & Beyond, Boyz Noize, Zeds Dead, and Steve Aoki, to name a few. Aoki, for example, started Dim Mak Records in 1996 to represent diverse EDM artists, such as Dada Life, the Bloody Beetroots, and Infected Mushroom; it now makes $16 million annually. Likewise, Diplo founded the Mad Decent label, which hosts Mad Decent Block Party concerts in nineteen cities and sells branded accessories and art.

Though not as famous as Diplo or Aoki, producer Reid Speed launched a smaller label to recognize emerging DJs. "I started my label (*Play Me Records*) to make a place for people who were otherwise getting hated on and turned down by other labels, just to give people a platform," she explains. "Big labels look to [us] to find whoever's going to be next. . . . If we're the people that can get you signed to [major labels] *Owsla*, *Mad Decent*, or *Atlantic*—then hell yeah!"[40] Efforts by record companies like these keep underground dance music going strong.

EDM artists also make their names and music prominent in everyday life by launching their own products. DJ branding has come a long way since the 1980s and 1990s, when artists made their logos and merchandise themselves. In 2012 Deadmau5 teamed up with Neff, a skateboard and snowboard apparel company, to design clothing that features his signature mouse helmet. "I love the street and snowboard scene," Deadmau5 explains. "The people involved [in that scene] are the people I see at my shows, so it made sense to hook up with a cool company like Neff."[41] More recently, Hardwell created a cologne called Eclipse in 2017, which introduces his name, his cologne, and his hit track (of the same name) into the fashion and lifestyle market.

Exposure on Every Channel

Another indication that EDM is firmly established in the mainstream is the fact that it routinely appears in commercials and on soundtracks.

Moby is one DJ who made waves when he became the first to license every track on his album *Play* (1999) to advertisers, TV producers, and filmmakers. This decision saved his album, which had sold only six thousand copies its first week and could not get radio play. Ten months later, however, people were hearing its tracks everywhere, including in Leonardo DiCaprio's popular movie *The Beach*. After that, the album sold 10 million copies. Companies began to realize that EDM was the perfect background music for everything from movies to shopping malls, not only because it was new and hip, but because it could also be multipurposed to fit any brand. As Gareth Grundy, a deputy editor at the London newspaper the *Observer*, puts it, "Thanks to vague or nonexistent lyrics, electronic music can mean almost anything to potential consumers."[42]

Nowhere has EDM's wide reach proved to be more apparent than in its appearance during the 2012 Super Bowl. The annual American football game attracted 111.3 million viewers and set a record for the most-watched US TV program ever. A Bud Light beer commercial that aired during the game depicted Avicii playing his track "Levels." Jocelyn Tannenbaum, a music journalist who writes about EDM, says, "The Super Bowl is known for having epic commercials so to feature an EDM track was a huge step for the genre."[43] The hit song was nominated for a Grammy, and later Bud Light ads featured Afrojack and Zedd. Since then, Diplo's "Express Yourself" has been highlighted in a Doritos ad; A-Trak and GTA's "Landline 2.0" has provided background music for an Adidas shoes spot, and vodka commercials have been set to dance tracks by Rüfüs du Sol and Galantis.

Even people who are not EDM fans are exposed to it regularly through the media. Songs by Flux Pavilion and Nero punched up the 2013 film *The Great Gatsby*; a Knife Party track was heard in the Emmy-winning TV series *Breaking Bad*; and a Lords of Acid song punctuated the movie trailer for the action fantasy *Sucker Punch* (2011). Notably, *Rolling Stone* has called rapper M.I.A.'s single with Diplo, "Paper Planes," the number two song of the century. The song took off after it was placed in the trailer for the comedy *Pineapple Express* in 2008. Dance tracks appear in video games, too. In addition to Marshmello's virtual concert during the game *Fortnite*, Deadmau5 stars in the virtual reality game *Absolut Deadmau5*, which debuted his song "Saved."

Perhaps most astoundingly, EDM has penetrated the political realm. In 1997 then-candidate for British prime minister Tony Blair surprised people when he used the dance track "Things Can Only Get Better" as his election campaign song. Written by admitted drug user Peter Cunnah, the track has been described as an ecstasy anthem. Whereas that song choice was controversial at the time, today using dance tracks for political purposes is normal. In fact, dubstep music featured prominently in a promo spot for President Barack Obama's 2013 State of the Union address, which is typically a very staid and dignified affair.

There is a dark side to EDM becoming mainstream, though. Star DJs are expected to produce music and tour at a frantic pace; for example, Steve Aoki played 198 gigs from June 2015 through May 2016, despite having throat surgery—typically he books 300 shows each year! Adding to the stress of jet-setting is nightly parties, where many producers are enticed by alcohol and drugs, resulting in substance abuse and consequent health problems.

Other disasters arise for fans when EDM gatherings get too big. In 2015, for example, transportation snafus at what was at the time North America's largest music festival, TomorrowWorld (held near Atlanta), left thousands of partygoers stranded overnight and sleeping in mud along the road. Worse, at Germany's

2010 Love Parade, improper crowd control of the 1.4 million at-tendees led to a stampede that killed 21 people and injured 650.

In response, music executives are recognizing there is more to event planning than booking a great lineup; meanwhile, some producers are slowing or halting their touring schedules. In 2013, for example, the trio that is Swedish House Mafia took a five-year hiatus due to, according to member Steve Angello, the pressure of playing big shows. In 2018 Hardwell, one of the world's top DJs, shocked fans when he also announced he was taking a break from performing.

Sounds of the Future

EDM has staying power because DJs continue to pioneer fresh sounds. Industry insiders predict the genre will see more future bass and African- and Asian-influenced sounds. Future bass was introduced by Australian producer Flume around 2006 but has recently exploded in popularity. Tunes by Marshmello, Louis the Child, Porter Robinson, Odezsa, and the two sisters who make up Krewella have propelled the genre forward. *Rolling Stone* even called future bass the EDM sound of 2017.

Now that club music has conquered the United States, art-ists are turning their attention to international audiences by incor-porating sounds from African, Japanese, or Korean pop (K-pop) music. For example, Andrew Taggart of the Chainsmokers col-laborated with K-pop superstars BTS on the single "Best of Me" in 2017. The song's release and photos of BTS with the Chain-smokers brought the latter new fans. It catapulted the DJs to the top ten on the Social 50 chart, which ranks musicians on the basis of their social media followers and interactions. Similarly, in 2019, Skrillex catered to Asian fans when he and Japanese songwriter Hikaru Utada created the opening theme song for the video game *Kingdom Hearts III*. With both Japanese and English versions, the track reached number one on iTunes in twenty-four world regions. Now some DJs are fusing Afrobeats, a drum-heavy style popular in Africa, with house music.

To keep EDM cutting-edge, savvy producers are turning their shows into live sets where they build part of the music in front of an audience. Glitch Mob, for instance, creates tracks on the fly using laptops and electronically connected instruments, such as drum machines. Another example is Canadian singer ill-esha, who sings vocals while playing records. This engages the audience and makes them feel like they are part of the music-making process. KJ Sawka, a member of the electronic bands Pendulum and Destroid, says, "Live EDM shows are gonna be bigger and bigger. More and more djs are gonna add live instruments to their show. The emotional connection is gonna be stronger than ever with fans."[44]

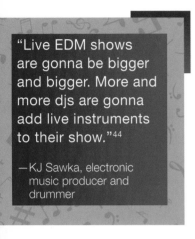

"Live EDM shows are gonna be bigger and bigger. More and more djs are gonna add live instruments to their show."[44]

—KJ Sawka, electronic music producer and drummer

The instrumental collaborations Sawka mentions are flourishing. The Colorado duo Big Gigantic create electronic music with live saxophone and drums; Pretty Lights, a DJ from Colorado, has guest keyboardists and drummers; Gramatik, from Slovenia, invites guitarists and other musicians onstage; and Stephan Bodzin, who won best Electronic Live Performer at the 2018 DJ Awards, DJed with a full marching band. In each case, live music brings the element of surprise and encourages fans to go and see their favorite artists perform more than once.

New Opportunities in the Industry

Though white male DJs have traditionally dominated the scene, doors are opening for female and black artists; for example, Black Coffee, a black DJ from South Africa, won Best Deep House at the DJ Awards three years in a row. Of *Mixmag's* top DJs of 2017, female Nina Kraviz and transgender African American Honey Dijon occupied the number one and two spots, respectively. In 2016, the Electric Daisy Carnival (EDC), an electronic music festival in Las Vegas that draws four hundred thousand attendees, booked Anna Lunoe and Alison Wonderland as headliners, the first solo women artists in the EDC's twenty-year history. Furthermore, EDM agencies are pledging to hire more female DJs and help close the gender gap between female and male artists' pay.

DJ Nina Kraviz performs at a festival in 2016. She was named the top DJ of 2017 by EDM magazine Mixmag.

These developments show that although electronic music has changed over the decades, it is firmly entrenched in all forms of music, as well as in mainstream daily life. Renowned artists keep up with trends—and form new ones as they take the genre in unexpected directions. Clearly, electronic music will remain a huge fixture of American culture, and fans will eagerly await the new sounds and other innovations EDM has in store.

$\mathcal{S}$OURCE NOTES

Introduction: By Young People, for Young People

1. Tom Breihan, "*Dig Your Own Hole* Turns 20," Stereogum, April 7, 2017. www.stereogum.com.
2. Bill Brewster and Frank Broughton, *Last Night a DJ Saved My Life*. New York: Grove Atlantic, 2007, p. 352.
3. Michaelangelo Matos, "How the Internet Transformed the American Rave Scene," *Record* (blog), National Public Radio, July 11, 2011. www.npr.org.
4. Arielle Castillo, Andrea Domanick, and Michaelangelo Matos, "50 Most Important People in EDM," *Rolling Stone*, March 17, 2014. www.rollingstone.com.

Chapter One: The Roots of EDM

5. Bill Brewster, "I Feel Love: Donna Summer and Giorgio Moroder Created the Template for Dance Music as We Know It," *Mixmag*, June 22, 2017. www.mixmag.net.
6. Jude Rogers, "Why Kraftwerk Are Still the World's Most Influential Band," *Guardian* (Manchester, UK), January 27, 2013. www.theguardian.com.
7. Quoted in Matthew Collin, *Rave On: Global Adventures in Electronic Dance Music*. Chicago: University of Chicago Press, 2018, p. 35.
8. Dom Phillips, "Trance-Mission," *Mixmag*, June 1992, p. 7.
9. Breihan, "*Dig Your Own Hole* Turns 20."
10. Quoted in Louis Pattison, "How the Political Warning of Autechre's Anti EP Made It a Warp Records Classic," *Vice*, July 21, 2014. www.vice.com.
11. Quoted in Stuart Aitken, "Mistletoe and Chime: The Story of Orbital's Acid House," *Guardian* (Manchester, UK), December 16, 2013. www.theguardian.com.

12. Mary Anne Hobbs, "Dubstep Warz," Mixcloud, January 9, 2011. www.mixcloud.com.

13. Quoted in Kate Hutchinson, "Sasha: 'There Were Thousands of People in Front of Me and I Was Losing the Plot,'" *Guardian* (Manchester, UK), April 12, 2016. www.theguardian.com.

Chapter Two: Dance Music Trendsetters

14. Lior Phillips, "The Past, Present, and Future of Daft Punk's *Homework*," *Consequence of Sound*, January 23, 2017. https://consequenceofsound.net.

15. Guy-Manuel de Homem-Christo and Thomas Bangalter, interviewed by Drew Tewksbury, "Daft Punk Pull Back the Curtain on 'Tron: Legacy' Soundtrack," *Hollywood Reporter*, December 16, 2010. www.hollywoodreporter.com.

16. Quoted in Mary Honeychild, "Preview of *Daft Punk Unchained* Documentary," *IDM Mag*, December 14, 2015. https://idm mag.com.

17. Tiësto, interviewed by Jordan Diaz, "Tiësto Talks Dance Music's Pop Makeover in Las Vegas & How Sven Väth Inspired His Career: Exclusive," *Billboard*, June 27, 2017. www.bill board.com.

18. Tiesto, "Tiesto: 'Why I Left Trance,'" YouTube video, *DJ Mag* TV, April 10, 2014. www.youtube.com.

19. Quoted in Charlotte Lucy Cijffers, "Martin Garrix: 'Tiësto Inspired Me to Get into Dance Music,'" *DJ Mag*, February 27, 2018. https://djmag.com.

20. Quoted in *Resident Advisor*, "Annie Mac: Biography," no date. www.residentadvisor.net.

21. Annie Mac, "Annie Mac: 'Time's Up for Male Dominated Live Music,'" *Grazia Daily*, February 6, 2018. https://graziadaily .co.uk.

22. androids, "The 15 Most Important Women in EDM," Complex, January 29, 2013. www.complex.com.

23. *Rolling Stone*, "The 25 DJs That Rule the Earth," November 9, 2012. www.rollingstone.com.

24. Sonny Moore (@Skrillex), "the underground drum and bass scene was getting at the time. He played 2 for me that I ended up buying that day: DJ Baron "Operation Pipe Dream" & Pendulum "Hold Your Color." I had already loved electronic music but after that day I told myself I would be a DJ," Twitter, June 8, 2018, 11:52 a.m. www.twitter.com.

25. Skrillex, "Grammys Live—Skrillex Accepting His First Grammy," YouTube video, CBS, February 12, 2012. www.youtube .com.

26. No Jumper Podcast, "The Diplo Interview," March 23, 2018. https://soundcloud.com.

Chapter Three: Building a Fan Base

27. Quoted in Anne Steele, "DJs Get Into Streaming Revenue Mix," *Wall Street Journal*, December 4, 2018. www.wsj.com.

28. Scott Wilson, "Apple Music Just Signed a Deal Transforming Online Mixes: What It Means for DJs and Dance Fans," *Fact Magazine*, March 16, 2016. www.factmag.com.

29. Rebekah Farrugia, *Beyond the Dance Floor: Female DJs, Technology, and Electronic Dance Music Culture*. Bristol, UK: Intellect, 2012, p. 43.

30. Quoted in *Rolling Stone*, "The 25 DJs That Rule the Earth."

31. Chris Comstock (@marshmellomusic), "What makes me happiest about today is that so many people got to experience their first concert ever. All the videos I keep seeing of people laughing and smiling throughout the set are amazing. Man I'm still so pumped," Twitter, February 2, 2019, 9:24 p.m. www .twitter.com.

32. Quoted in Kat Bein, "Afrojack Launches 'Global Remix Battle' to Find New Talent," *Billboard*, September 24, 2018. www. billboard.com.

33. Jace Clayton, *Uproot: Travels in 21st-Century Music and Digital Culture*. New York: Farrar, Straus and Giroux, 2016, p. 145.

34. Quoted in Emilee Lindner, "How Did the Chainsmokers, of All People, End Up Dominating 2016?," Noisey, *Vice*, December 30, 2016. https://noisey.vice.com.

35. Quoted in Stevo Jacobs, "24 Music Industry Predictions for 2019," EDM Sauce, December 14, 2018. www.edmsauce .com.

Chapter Four: EDM Is Here to Stay

36. Quoted in Jacobs, "24 Music Industry Predictions for 2019."
37. Matthew Meadow, "Borgore Drops 6-Track Jazz Album, 'Adventures in Time,'" YourEDM, May 9, 2018. www.youredm .com.
38. Ezra Marcus, "What's Underneath Dance Music's Big Tent?," Vulture, September 20, 2017. www.vulture.com.
39. Lindsey Stirling, interviewed by Kristen Philipkoski, "Why Not Winning *America's Got Talent* and Avoiding a Major Record Label Was Awesome for Lindsey Stirling," *Forbes*, August 31, 2015. www.forbes.com.
40. Reid Speed, interviewed by Grace Kelly, "Reid Speed: Sorry Not Sorry," Bullet Music, November 29, 2016. www.bullet music.net.
41. Devon Maloney, "Deadmau5 Teams Up with Neff for Hat and Hoodie Line," *Spin*, July 26, 2012. www.spin.com.
42. Gareth Grundy, "Moby Licenses Every Track on *Play*. Ker-Ching!" *Guardian* (Manchester, UK), June 14, 2011. www .theguardian.com.
43. Jocelyn Tannenbaum, "EDM Takes Over Commercials," iEDM, August 6, 2016. https://iedm.com.
44. Quoted in Jacobs, "24 Music Industry Predictions for 2019."

*F*OR FURTHER RESEARCH

Books

Jace Clayton, *Uproot: Travels in 21st-Century Music and Digital Culture*. New York: Farrar, Straus and Giroux, 2016.

Rebekah Farrugia, *Beyond the Dance Floor: Female DJs, Technology, and Electronic Dance Music Culture*. Bristol, UK: Intellect, 2012.

Michaelangelo Matos, *The Underground Is Massive: How Electronic Dance Music Conquered America*. New York: Dey Street, 2015.

Internet Sources

Joseph L. Flatley, "Beyond Lies the Wub: A History of Dubstep," Verge, August 28, 2012. www.theverge.com.

Guardian (Manchester, UK), "A History of Dance Music," June 14, 2011. www.theguardian.com.

Stevo Jacobs, "24 Music Industry Predictions for 2019," EDM Sauce, December 14, 2018. www.edmsauce.com.

Ezra Marcus, "What's Underneath Dance Music's Big Tent?," Vulture, September 20, 2017. www.vulture.com.

Anne Steele, "DJs Get Into Streaming Revenue Mix," *Wall Street Journal*, December 4, 2018. www.wsj.com.

Thump Staff, "The 101 Best EDM Songs of All Time," Noisey, *Vice*, July 12, 2017. https://noisey.vice.com.

Kevin Watson, *IMS Business Report 2018*. Ibiza, Spain: International Music Summit, May 23–25, 2018. www.internationalmusic summit.com.

Websites

DJ Mag (www.djmag.com). Founded as a print magazine in the United Kingdom in 1991, *DJ Mag* now also represents electronic music worldwide through its website, YouTube channel, and the music events it hosts. Each year hundreds of thousands of readers vote in its famed Top 100 clubs list, Top 100 DJs list, and Best of British Awards to recognize UK acts.

EDM.com (www.edm.com). Designed for both fans and industry insiders around the world, EDM.com publishes news, music reviews, interviews, and editorials about modern electronic music, such as "Analyzing the State of the EDM Album in 2018."

Red Bull Music Academy (www.redbullmusicacademy.com). The music academy hosts music workshops, lectures, and festivals internationally. It publishes in-depth information about music history, including a series of articles on the birth of techno and the rise of house, and features on electronic music artists such as Jeff Mills, Egyptian Lover, and Tiga.

Resident Advisor (www.residentadvisor.net). Since 2001, this online magazine and platform provides electronic music news, reviews, history, and artists' biographies. On the site, visitors can browse job openings, music videos, podcasts, and documentaries.

Your EDM (www.youredm.com). Covering multiple subgenres of house and bass music, Your EDM offers dance music news, event photos, the Aspire to Inspire series of interviews with industry professionals, and free music downloads.

INDEX

PICTURE CREDITS

ABOUT THE AUTHOR

Jamuna Carroll is a writer, editor, and performer in San Diego, California. Her writing has been published in more than forty non-fiction books, including *Strange Science*, *Facts to Annoy Your Teacher*, and *Thinking Critically: Social Networking*. She has been a fan of electronic music since the 1990s and has interviewed acclaimed DJs, including the Grammy-winning DJ duo Deep Dish.